SO-AUX-471

7043
978
KAZ

DATE DUE

E. GALARZA ELEMENTARY SCHOOL
1610 Bird Ave.
San Jose, CA 95125

Hammer

Historical Etchings

Frontier Life

51428

Copyright-free illustrations for lovers of history

Compiled by
Bobbie Kalman

🌳 **Crabtree Publishing Company**

Historical Etchings Series

In 19th-century North America, hundreds of artists produced black-and-white steel-plate and woodcut engravings for newspapers, periodicals, books, and catalogs. Over a period of more than five years, Bobbie Kalman and Peter Crabtree traveled to libraries throughout North America to research these etchings for Crabtree Publishing Company's *Early Settler Life* series. Researching etchings meant working in climate-controlled rooms to make sure the pages of the old newspapers and books in which these etchings appeared did not crumble due to age and dryness. Special photographers had to be hired and approved.

Many of the etchings in the *Early Settler Life* series have never appeared in other collections, so Bobbie is often asked for permission to use them. By popular demand, they have been gathered into a series of their own: the *Historical Etchings* series. Today, although many of the original sources and creators' names are forgotten, these illustrations offer a fascinating glimpse into the daily lives of the people who settled North America.

Crabtree Publishing Company

350 Fifth Avenue	360 York Road, RR 4	73 Lime Walk
Suite 3308	Niagara-on-the-Lake	Headington
New York	Ontario, Canada	Oxford OX3 7AD
N.Y. 10118	L0S 1J0	United Kingdom

Copyright © **1998 CRABTREE PUBLISHING COMPANY.**
The illustrations may be used, free and without permission, provided that no more than fifteen appear in the same publication or project. Rights to the illustrations may not be rented, transferred, or granted to another person or organization. The illustrations may not be used to embarrass or defame any person or entity. This book may not be copied in its entirety. The text that accompanies the illustrations may not be reproduced in any form without the written permission of Crabtree Publishing Company.

Cataloging in Publication Data

Kalman, Bobbie
    Frontier life: copyright-free illustrations for lovers of history

(Historical etchings)

ISBN 0-86505-914-4 (pbk.)
This book contains etchings and accompanying text depicting various aspects of frontier life, including homes, hunting, and frontier towns.

1. Frontier and pioneer life—North America—Pictorial works—Juvenile literature. 2. North America—Social life and customs—Pictorial works—Juvenile literature. [1. Frontier and pioneer life. 2. North America—Social life and customs.] I. Title. II. Series: Kalman, Bobbie. Historical etchings.

E179.5.K353 1997   j978   LC 97-37455

CIP

Contents

As her husband chops trees to clear the land, this young settler wife gathers firewood. Fire was the only source of heat and light in an early settler's home, which was a one-room log cabin.

*B*efore their home was built, settler families camped in the wilderness. Everything, including cooking, was done outdoors. Meals were prepared over a small, open fire.

It was too hot to cook inside the one-room house in the summer. Many families built an outdoor oven in which to do their cooking, but this family does not have one yet. The sons prepare a fire on which dinner will be made.

Pioneers used whatever materials they found for construction. Birch bark was peeled from trees and collected to make canoes or shelters. It was also used to make roofs for cabins.

This settler uses a sledge and oxen to haul logs that have been cut to extend his fence. He does this work over the winter, when there is not much other work to do.

These men are heading to the field in a stoneboat. They will load it with the rocks they clear from the land. When the stoneboat is full, the men will take it to the middle of the field where they will pile up the rocks.

This farmer is clearing the land around his house. After he finishes chopping down the trees, he must pull out the stumps. He will use a horse or ox for this heavy work. It will be years before his fields are clear.

The frontier homestead was a small, simple shack made of logs or sod. Family members lived in this small house until they had to move or could afford to build a larger home.

After working hard all day, families often gathered around the fireplace to relax. Storytelling was a pastime that everyone enjoyed. Parents told their children about the family they had left behind.

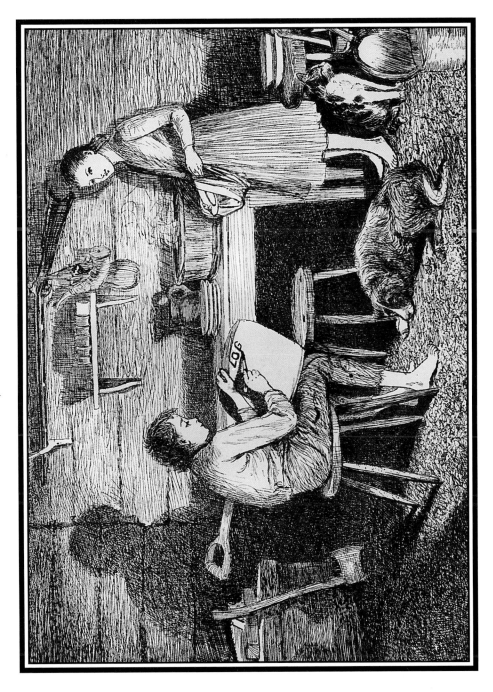

There were few schools on the frontier. Most children studied at home when they weren't busy working. They learned the basics of reading, writing, and arithmetic.

Settlers on the frontier hunted wild animals for food and clothing. These hunters will share the moose that they have killed. The meat will provide their families with a few hearty meals, and the hide will be used to make clothing.

This bear had been prowling around the homestead for weeks. Everyone is relieved that it has been caught. The family no longer has to worry about having their food stolen. Father will share the meat and fur with the neighbor who helped him hunt the bear. Every part of the animal was used.

Boys learned to hunt and trap at an early age. These two are hoping to catch
a rabbit in the trap they set the night before. Their parents will be happy to have
extra meat.

*I*n winter, food often was scarce. This settler and his son were lucky to catch
an opossum and some rabbits. The animals will make enough stew to last
several days!

Can you guess what this woman is trying to keep out? It is a hungry bear like the one shown on the opposite page!

This bear can smell wonderful foods inside the smoke house, but the settler doesn't feel like sharing!

Many men ventured into the wilderness to trap animals for their fur. These trappers needed a place to trade or sell their pelts, and trading posts sprang up on the frontier. Many of the trading posts were run by large European companies.

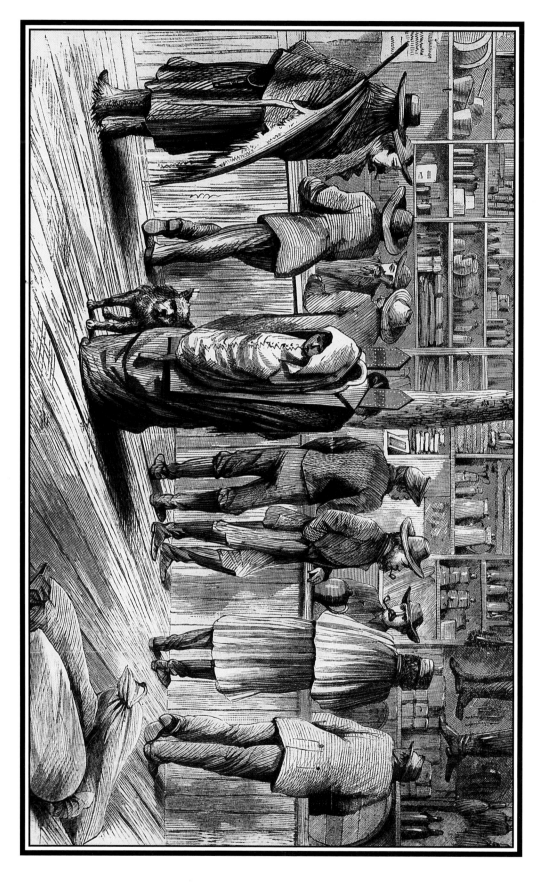

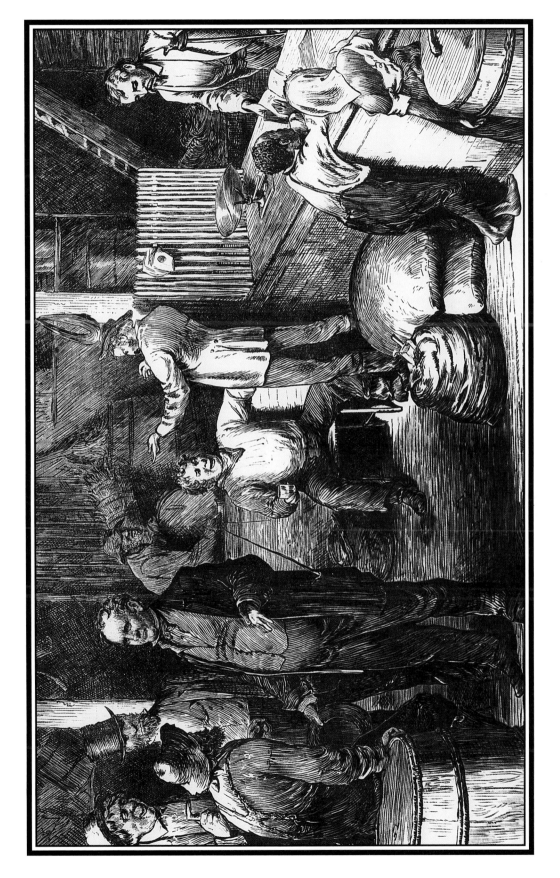

As more people settled in an area, general stores appeared. The store carried goods that most people could not grow or make themselves, such as coffee, spices, shoes, pots and pans, and medicines. Most people bartered, or traded, for the goods at the store.

*B*efore beginning their long journey west, people prepared their wagons and gathered food, water, and other supplies in a frontier town. They met others who were heading west, and together they formed a wagon train.

This girl went for a horseback ride when the wagon train stopped for the day.
Her father waves to her to come back because she is riding in unfamiliar territory.
He also wants the horse to have a rest after carrying a heavy load all day.

In the mid-1800s, pioneers began leaving towns and cities in the east to head west, where they could get free land. Although they had wagons, most people walked the 2000 miles to California or Oregon. With little grass or water, their horses were often too weak and tired to pull the extra weight of passengers.

*L*ife on some parts of the westward trail was hot, dusty, and dull. Pioneers traveled for days without seeing trees, animals, or other people. Sometimes the heat and boredom was so unbearable that people got sick or simply fell asleep.

As more and more people moved west, villages and towns grew on the frontier. Some areas of the west attracted large numbers of people very quickly. Boomtowns like the one in the bottom picture sprang up in these busy places.

Winter was an easy time for settlers to travel the long distance from their homestead to the town. Even if a family did not own a sleigh, people could ski or snowshoe over ground that was rough and muddy the rest of the year.

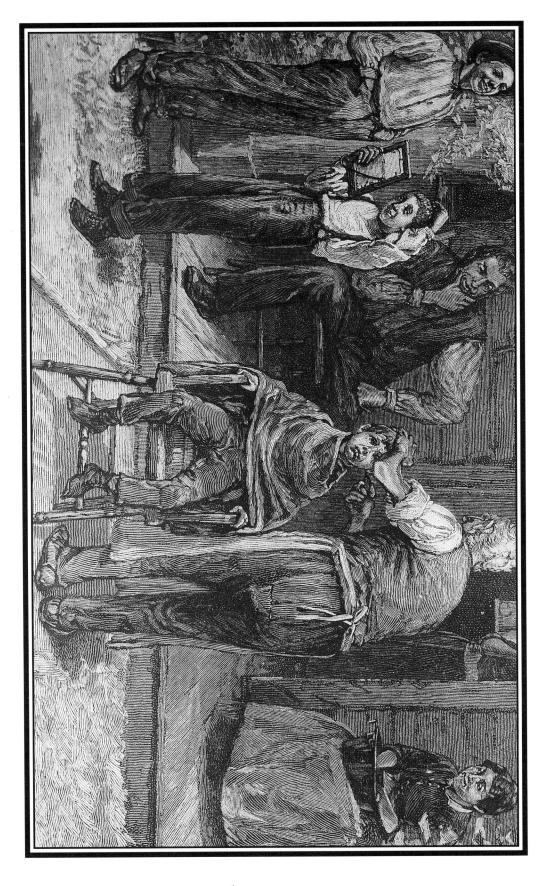

*B*efore moving to the frontier, grandpa was a barber in a city back east. He made a decent living there. These days, he gives free haircuts to people in town in exchange for extra food or other goods.

In most frontier towns, people did not have money to spend on unnecessary things such as photographs. Photographers, artists, and other people whose services were a luxury did not stay in one town for long. They traveled from place to place to find settlers with enough money to pay for their services.

Circuit doctors traveled from town to town to treat the sick and injured. There were always a lot of patients to be found along the frontier. Doctors often treated livestock as well as human patients.

*F*armers kept the local blacksmith busy making and repairing their tools and implements. While they waited, they exchanged news and gossip and enjoyed some fiddle tunes.

The settlers who lived in this cold, western community built sturdy, walled forts that kept out enemies. They used dog sleds for travel.